Sit in!

Written by Clare Helen Welsh

Illustrated by Julia Seal

Collins

Sit in Sam.

2

Sam sits in.

Sit in Sid.

Sid sits in.

Sit in Nad.

Nad sits in.

Sit in Pam.

Sit in Tam.

Pam sits in.

Tam sits in.

11

Sit in Sam.

Sam sits in.

/n/

14

After reading

Letters and Sounds: Phase 2

Word count: 36

Focus phonemes: /s/ /a/ /t/ /p/ /i/ /n/ /m/ /d/

Curriculum links: Shape, space and measures

Early learning goals: Reading: read and understand simple sentences; use phonic knowledge to decode regular words and read them aloud accurately

Developing fluency

- Your child may enjoy hearing you read the book.
- Take turns to read Sam's (the girl's) words (pages 4, 6 and 8) in a friendly way as she invites her friends to sit in the car.
- Take turns to use a different voice for the narrator.

Phonic practice

- Say the word **Sit** on page 6. Ask your child to say it too, encouraging them to sound out each letter (s/i/t) first, then blending.
- Turn to page 10 and ask your children to sound out **sits** (s/i/t/s) and then blend.
- On pages 12 and 13, focus on the words **sit** and **sits**. Ask your child to sound out and blend these two words, checking they don't forget the additional /s/ in **sits**.
- Look at the "I spy sounds" pages (14 and 15). Point to the nose of the boy near the mirror and say: "nose", emphasising the /n/ sound. Ask your child to find more things that contain the /n/ sound. (*nurse, necklace, numbers, nine, net, neck, notepad, nap, noise, notes, noticeboard, noodles*) Point out how some things might have the /n/ in the middle or at the end. (e.g. *sniff, dance, pan, sun, wand*)

Extending vocabulary

- On page 6, discuss what Sam could say instead of "Sit in Nad"? (e.g. *Jump in Nad; Get in Nad; Come in Nad*)
- On page 11, discuss what the narrator could say instead of "Tam sits in"? (e.g. *Tam gets in; Tam climbs in; Tam squeezes in*)